*W*ithin you is an ideal,
a voice of youth,
and a promise of achievement
still to come.
Within your hands
are special gifts and talents.
Within your mind is the
source of your dreams…
Within you is the promise
of the future,
and I believe in you.

— Jean Lamey

Other books in the *"Language of"* Series...

Blue Mountain Arts®

The Language of Courage and Inner Strength

The Language of Friendship

The Language of Happiness

The Language of Love

The Language of Marriage

The Language of Positive Thinking

The Language of Prayer

The Language of Recovery

The Language of Success

The Language of Teaching

Thoughts to Share with a Wonderful Mother

Thoughts to Share with a Wonderful Father

Thoughts to Share with a Wonderful Son

Thoughts to Share with a Wonderful Daughter

It's Great to Have a Brother like You

It's Great to Have a Sister like You

☆

The Language of

TEENAGERS

Words to Remember

A Blue Mountain Arts® Collection

Blue Mountain Press ®

SPS Studios, Inc., Boulder, Colorado

Library of Congress Catalog Card Number: 00-037153
ISBN: 1-58786-000-7

ACKNOWLEDGMENTS appear on page 48.

Certain trademarks are used under license.

Manufactured in Thailand
First Printing: April 2000

♻ This book is printed on recycled paper.

Library of Congress Cataloging-in-Publication Data

The language of teenagers.
    p.   cm.
  ISBN 1-58786-000-7 (alk. paper)
  1. Conduct of life--Quotations, maxims, etc. I. SPS Studios.
  PN6084.C556 L38 2000
  082--dc21

00-037153

SPS Studios, Inc.

P.O. Box 4549, Boulder, Colorado 80306

Contents

(Authors listed in order of first appearance)

"For My Teenager"
Words I Want You to Remember

I can barely begin to tell you of all my wishes for you • There are so many of them, and I want them all to come true • I want you to use your heart as a compass as you grow and find your way in the world, but I want you to always have an appreciation for the direction of home • I want you to be self-reliant, self-motivated, and self-sufficient, but to know that you will never be alone • I want you to be safe and smart and cautious • I want you to be wise beyond your years • I don't want you to grow up too fast • I want you to come to me with your fears •

I want the people who share your days to realize that they are in the presence of a very special someone • You are a wonderful, rare person with no comparison • I want you to know that opportunities will come, and you'll have many goals to achieve • The more that obstacles get in the way of your dreams, the more you'll need to believe • Get your feet wet with new experiences, but be sure you never get in over your head •

I want you to realize how capable you are, and that your possibilities are unlimited ⋄ I hope you never lose your childlike wonder, your delight and appreciation in interesting things ⋄ I know you'll keep responding in a positive way to the challenges life always brings ⋄ I pray that you won't rush the future, and that you'll slowly build on the steppingstones of the past ⋄ You have a strong foundation of family and friends and joy that will always last ⋄

I wish I could find the words to tell you how much I love you each and every day ⋄ But that feeling is so strong and its meaning is so magnificent, it can be hard to know just what to say ⋄

I love you beyond all words ⋄ And I promise that I will love you beyond all time ⋄ So many treasures await you in your journey of life...

and being blessed with you... has been mine ⋄

 Douglas Pagels

In Case I Haven't Told You Lately...
I'm Proud of You,
My Child

Many days go by
and I find myself saying
the same things to you
day in and day out:
"Clean your room."
"Is your room clean?"
"Do your homework."
"Did you finish your homework?"
"Don't be late."
"Take the trash out, please..."

Many nights, after you have
fallen asleep and look so peaceful,
I have wondered to myself...
Did I tell you that I love you?
That I appreciate all you do for me?
That through your entire life
you will find me in your cheering section?

Have I asked you lately
    about your happiness
and what's going on in your life?

I am sorry that there are so many times
when I get caught up with
the everyday routines
that I forget the simple,
important things in life.
I hope that you will forgive me
for my shortcomings,
as I will forgive you.
Always remember that
no matter how busy I seem to be,
I love you very much,
and I am proud of all that you do
and all that you stand for.

☆ Toni Crossgrove Shippen

A wonderful realization will be the day you realize that you are unique in all the world. There is nothing that is an accident. You are a special combination for a purpose — and don't let them tell you otherwise, even if they tell you that purpose is an illusion.... You are that combination so that you can do what is essential for you to do. Don't ever believe that you have nothing to contribute. The world is an incredible unfulfilled tapestry, and only you can fulfill the tiny space that is yours.

Leo Buscaglia

A Motto for Teenagers

Be an independent thinker
Make decisions
based on how you feel
and on what you know is right
regardless of what your peers
or other people think
Know yourself
Know what you can
and want to do in life
Set goals
and work hard to achieve them
Have fun every day in every way
Be creative —
it is an expression of your feelings
Be sensitive in viewing the world
Trust in your family
Believe in love —
it is the most complete
and important emotion possible
Believe in yourself
and know that you are loved

Susan Polis Schutz

Take These Thoughts with You on Your Journey Through Life

Don't ever forget that you are unique.
Be your best self
and not an imitation of someone else.
Find your strengths
and use them in a positive way.
Don't listen to those
who ridicule the choices you make.
Travel the road that you have chosen
and don't look back with regret.
You have to take chances
to make your dreams happen.
Remember that there is plenty of time
to travel another road — and still another —
in your journey through life.
Take the time to find the route
that is right for you.

You will learn something valuable
from every trip you take,
so don't be afraid to make mistakes.
Tell yourself that you're okay
just the way you are.
Make friends who respect your true self.
Take the time to be alone, too,
so you can know just how terrific
your own company can be.
Remember that being alone
doesn't always mean being lonely;
it can be a beautiful experience
of finding your creativity,
your heartfelt feelings,
and the calm and quiet peace deep inside you.

Please don't ever forget that you are special
and very much loved.

Jacqueline Schiff

Definition of a Successful Life

To laugh often and much;
to win the respect of intelligent people
and the affection of children;
to earn the appreciation of honest critics
and endure the betrayal of false friends;
to appreciate beauty, to find the best in others;
to leave the world a bit better,
whether by a healthy child,
a garden patch or a redeemed social condition;
to know even one life has breathed easier
because you have lived.

☆ Ralph Waldo Emerson

Very little is needed to make a happy life.
It is all within yourself.

☆ Marcus Aurelius

It's a funny thing about life;
if you refuse to accept
anything but the best,
you very often get it.

Somerset Maugham

It is so important
to choose your own
lifestyle
and not let others
choose it for you

Susan Polis Schutz

The grand essentials
to happiness
in this life are
something to do
something to love
and something
        to hope for.

Joseph Addison

Be glad of life
because it gives
you the chance
to love and to work
and to play and to
look up at the stars.

Henry van Dyke

Happiness cannot come from without. It must come from within. It is not what we see and touch or that which others do for us which makes us happy; it is that which we think and feel and do, first for the other fellow and then for ourselves.

Helen Keller

Happiness resides not in possessions and not in gold, the feeling of happiness dwells in the soul.

Democritus

Joy is not in things; it is in us.

Richard Wagner

No Matter What Choices
You Make in Life,
You're Still a Part of Me

Your choices in life are so different from
    what I would have chosen for you
I dreamed so many dreams for you
I wanted your life to be perfect
And I guess I forgot whose life it was
I guess I forgot they were my dreams — not yours
You have learned so many things the hard way
But I guess that's the only way you knew how to learn
I want you to know that even though you've
    chosen your own path to follow
I will always be there to love and support you
I know I won't always agree with you
But I also know that I have to let you figure
    things out for yourself
It's hard for me to let go
And it's hard for me to let you make mistakes
But I know you are a strong and capable person
And in the end you will triumph
Because even though you are your own person
You're still a part of me

                        Judy LeSage

An Affirmation for Teenagers

I communicate freely.

It is safe for me to grow up. I love to learn and grow and change, and I feel safe in the midst of it all, knowing that change is a natural part of life. My personality is flexible, and it is easy for me to go with the flow of life. My inner being is consistent; therefore, I am safe in every kind of experience. When I was a little child, I did not know what the future would bring. As I now begin my journey into adulthood, I realize that tomorrow is equally unknown and mysterious. I choose to believe that it is safe for me to grow up and take charge of my life. My first adult act is to learn to love myself unconditionally, for then I can handle whatever the future may bring.

Louise L. Hay

Thoughts from the Heart
of a Teenager

Give us our little wishes, our own clothes, our harmless rebellions. The chance to make our own mistakes, to grow our special gardens. Tolerate our musings, as we learn and change our minds. Don't lead or we won't learn to walk alone, to see, or speak our minds.

Listen before you judge us; we feel deeply and have reasons, too. Remember we must chase different dreams before we find what we best can do.

Trust our actions and our choices,
however different from your own.
Give us the courage to take chances,
to know if we fall we are not alone.
Have patience with our yearnings as
we see our intentions through. Let
us know that where we are coming
from is a safe place to return to.

Allow us the freedom to be creative,
the opportunity to be wrong. Teach
us that we don't have to be perfect
to belong. Give us our secret plans,
our own music, our space to grow.
Learn with us as we discover these
things. When the time is right, let
us go.

 Ashley Rice

A Teenager Is...

...the one who taught me — constantly — of my capacity to love, to experience life in its most meaningful way, and to open my heart wide enough to let all those joyful feelings inside.

Laurel Atherton

...an ideal,
a voice of youth,
and a promise of achievement
still to come.

Jean Lamey

...a vast assortment of contradictions and contrasts. As they strive to discover who they are and where they want to go in life, they go through identities as easily as changing their clothes. However, they all share a common goal: to become adults capable of fulfilling all their childhood dreams.

Mary Booker Edwards

...part of a generation that stands at a unique moment in the history of the world. Their dreams are deeper; their emotions are stronger; their energy is greater. Each teenager has the opportunity and the potential to change the world for the better.

Edmund O'Neill

...the hopes and dreams of a weary adult world reborn again, with clear eyes, shining hopes, and a bright path to the future.

Eloise Lang

...the sparkle in my eyes
and the pride in my heart...
the courage that gives me strength
and the love that gives me life...
my inspiration
and the best gift I ever received.

Lois Carruthers

A Teenager Is...

...a person who is part child and part adult.
...someone who loves to have fun
and thrives on excitement,
yet sometimes feels overwhelmed by
new responsibilities and expectations.
...someone who is still learning from the past
and is unsure about the future.
...someone who craves friends and
    an active social life, yet finds that
    you can't please everyone.
...someone who needs someone
    in his or her life
who is a good example,
who can be trusted with secrets,
who is an avid listener.
...someone who needs to know
    that life always gets better
and that things worth having
are worth working and waiting for.

A teenager is someone who needs to understand that
trying, combined with persistence and determination,
are the biggest parts of succeeding
and that mistakes are okay
as long as you learn from them.

In between the joy of being a protected,
    cherished child
and the contentment of being a free,
    independent adult
is the fun
the frustration
the confusion
the boredom
the excitement
the despondence
and the elation
of a
teenager.

Barbara Cage

Accept Yourself

We need to accept ourselves, just as we accept the color of our eyes. They're either brown, blue, green, or some variation. One color is not better or worse. They are all beautiful, and we wouldn't try to change them.

Our personalities are developed from influences, such as family, society, schools, and church. We are the result of all that has collected on us to make us unique. Much like the color of our eyes, our ways are set. This doesn't mean we should not try to change something that we really want to change, but, rather, it is about using acceptance as a catalyst to make changes happen. If we're in a state of acceptance, there is more freedom of choice and, therefore, a better opportunity to succeed.

Ask yourself these questions: Is putting myself down getting the job done? Do I respond better to criticism or acceptance? Am I more motivated by turmoil or ease? Do I find it easier to do something if I *have to* or just *want to*? How long have I been trying to make this change using the same tactics I've been using?

Sometimes listening to your own answers is more helpful than "should have's" or "could have's." As you search to get along better in life and try to understand your own nature and resistance to change, maybe you need to hear more acceptance of yourself than reprimands.

Criticism often takes away the freedom to choose to do something. Acceptance helps us believe we can change or do something we want to. Sometimes we need to take off our running shoes and boxing gloves and stop the lectures and criticisms. We need approval and acceptance of our imperfections, the same kind of simple acceptance we have for the color of our eyes.

You're good, unique, and special.
Accept yourself!

Donna Fargo

It isn't your background, your heritage,
   or your culture
that others admire most in you;
it isn't the way you dress,
   how you look,
or what you have.
It's something inside of you
that says to the world,
"I'm worth knowing... I have so much
   to give.
I love being me, for I'm someone
   special in this life —
someone you'd be proud to know."

Barbara J. Hall

Greatness is not found in possessions,
power, position or prestige. It is discovered
in goodness, humility, service and character.

William Ward

There is only one success — to be able to spend your life in your own way.

Christopher Morley

You've got to be real. Don't be a phony. Come on as yourself. The hardest thing in the world is to be something you're not. As you get closer and closer and closer to what you are, be that, and come on all the time that way. You'll find it's an easy way to live. The easiest thing to be in the world is you. The most difficult thing to be is what other people want you to be. Don't let them put you in that position. Find "you," who you are, come on as you are. Then you can live simply.

Leo Buscaglia

We need to feel more
to understand others
We need to love more
to be loved back
We need to cry more
to cleanse ourselves
We need to laugh more
to enjoy ourselves

We need to establish the values of honesty
    and fairness
when interacting with people
We need to establish a strong ethical basis
as a way of life

We need to see more
other than our own little fantasies
We need to hear more
and listen to the needs of others

We need to give more
and take less
We need to share more
and own less
We need to realize the importance of the family
as a backbone to stability
We need to look more
and realize that we are not so different from
    one another

We need to create a world where
we can all peacefully live
the life we choose
We need to create a world where
we can trust each other

Susan Polis Schutz

Some Thoughts
About How to Resolve
Disagreements in Your Life

Whenever you become involved
in a confrontation,
it's best to allow yourself
some time to really think about
all sides of the situation.
Before becoming defensive,
give yourself the opportunity
    to be receptive.
Remember that all problems have more
    than one answer;
there are always
    extenuating circumstances
for everyone to consider.

Be willing to listen;
    be open to the possibility
that things can be worked out,
because you can reach a compromise
    out of any conclusion.
Before you enter into
    a major debate,
take time to compose
    your thoughts and feelings.
Realize that anything
    and everything in life
has its own unique perspective,
and before you jump
    to any conclusions,
it's important to allow yourself
the time to completely understand.

Deanna Beisser

Remember the Importance of Friendship

Much certainty of the happiness and purity of our lives depends on our making a wise choice of our companions and friends.

John Lubbock

True happiness consists not in the multitude of friends, but in their worth and choice.

Ben Jonson

The happiest moments my heart knows are those in which it is pouring forth its affections to a few esteemed characters.

Thomas Jefferson

Some people will be your friend
because of whom you know
Some people will be your friend
because of your position
Some people will be your friend
because of the way you look
Some people will be your friend
because of your possessions
But the only real friends
are the people who will be your friends
because they like you for how you are inside

Susan Polis Schutz

Don't Walk Alone
Through Life

The world is too big a place
to walk through alone.
There are too many city streets
    and too many dirt roads.
There are too many hours
    to fill by yourself,
and too many empty moments.
There are too many lonely hearts
    that need to be loved,
too many strangers that need
    to be welcomed,
too many people who are in need
    and should be helped,
and too many things to share.

One person alone might take
    for granted something
that two or more people together
    learn to appreciate.
There are too many stars
    to count by yourself
and too many birds to feed.

If you walk alone,
who will be there to answer the phone
when you decide to call?
Who will grasp your hand
    when you reach out?
Who will pick up the pieces
    if your world were to fall apart?
Time is too short
to not reach out to others.
Don't walk alone.

Kelly D. Caron

Reach for Your Dreams...

Many people speak of dreams as fanciful things like fairies and charmed rings and lands of enchantment. Others only believe in faraway dreams such as stars or sea castles with elf-like inhabitants.

There are day-dreamers and night-dreamers who dream up make-believe places. They use much imagination, and in that are dream-gifted. But the serious dreamers are those who catch dreams to bring them to life, and show that when they were dreaming, they meant it.

☆ Ashley Rice

To accomplish great things, we must not only act but also dream, not only plan but also believe.

☆ Anatole France

If you want a thing bad enough
To go out and fight for it,
Work day and night for it,
Give up your time and your peace and your sleep for it,
If only desire of it
Makes you quite mad enough
Never to tire of it,
Makes you hold all other things tawdry and cheap for it,
If life seems all empty and useless without it
And all that you scheme and you dream is about it,
If gladly you'll sweat for it,
Fret for it,
Plan for it,
Lose all your terror of God or man for it,
If you'll simply go after that thing that you want,
With all your capacity,
Strength and sagacity,
Faith, hope and confidence, stern pertinacity,
If neither cold poverty, famished and gaunt,
Nor sickness nor pain
Of body or brain
Can turn you away from the thing that you want,
If dogged and grim you besiege and beset it,
You'll get it!

Berton Braley

Enthusiasm is one of the most powerful engines of success. When you do a thing, do it with all your might.... Be active, be energetic, be enthusiastic and faithful, and you will accomplish your objective.

Ralph Waldo Emerson

Whatever you can do or dream you can do, begin it. Boldness has genius and magic and power in it.

Johann Wolfgang von Goethe

The future belongs to those who believe in the beauty of their dreams.

Marie Curie

To be what we are, and to become what we
are capable of becoming is the only end of life.

Robert Louis Stevenson

The best gift possible
is to hand yourself,
every morning,
three-hundred
and sixty-five
new and unused days,
any one of which
may turn out to be
the best day
you ever had
in your life.

Ellis Parker Butler

Look to the Future...

Your success and happiness lie in you.
External conditions are the accidents of life, its
outer trappings. The great, enduring realities are
love and service. Joy is the holy fire that keeps
our purpose warm and our intelligence aglow.
Resolve to keep happy, and your joy and you
shall form an invincible host against difficulty.

Helen Keller

No bird soars too high,
if he soars with his own wings.

William Blake

My challenge to the young people
is to pick up where this generation has
left off, to create a world where every
man, woman and child is not limited,
except by their own capabilities.

Colin Powell

You have powers you never dreamed of.
You can do things you never thought you
could do. There are no limitations in what
you can do except the limitations in your
own mind as to what you cannot do.
Don't think you cannot.
Think you can.

Darwin P. Kingsley

May All Your Dreams
Come True

Lean against a tree
and dream your world of dreams
Work hard at what you like to do
and try to overcome all obstacles
Laugh at your mistakes
and praise yourself for learning from them
As you go through life
pick some flowers
and appreciate the beauty of nature
Be honest with people
and enjoy the good in them

Don't be afraid to show your emotions
Laughing and crying make you feel better
Love your friends and family
     with your entire being
They are the most important part of your life
Feel the calmness on a quiet sunny day
and plan what you want to accomplish in life
Find a rainbow
and live your
world of dreams
I love you

Susan Polis Schutz

To My Teenager

...As Long as We
Remain Open with Each Other,
We'll Grow Together

I know sometimes you think I don't understand you,
but I do remember how difficult being a teenager is.
I know it is not easy working through
all the feelings you are experiencing,
and I hope that you will always feel free
to turn to me about any subject.

Your teenage years should be filled
with wonderful experiences,
and I want all the times in your life
to be fulfilling and enjoyable.
I know sometimes you think
I am being too nosy about your private life,
or I am telling you what to do,
but I am not trying to make you feel as if
you have no independence.

I know you need your own space at times,
and I understand you need room to grow.
But as your parent, I want you to be healthy and happy
and have every opportunity in life you deserve.
When I put my foot down
or make a few rules for you to follow,
I'm doing what I think is best for you.

Still, I want us always to be able
to work through any of our differences
and communicate openly with each other.
Just as any relationship has its ups and downs,
so will ours as parent and child.
We have always had a good relationship,
and I think we can grow and learn together
in all the years ahead if we both work hard
at listening and respecting each other.
You are very important to me.
I hope you know I love you with all my heart,
and I am proud to be your parent.

Susan Hickman Sater

ACKNOWLEDGMENTS

We gratefully acknowledge the permission granted by the following authors, publishers, and authors' representatives to reprint poems or excerpts from their publications.

Leo F. Buscaglia, Inc. for "A wonderful realization..." and "You've got to be real...." from LIVING, LOVING & LEARNING by Leo Buscaglia, Ph.D., published by Ballantine Books. Copyright © 1982 by Leo F. Buscaglia, Inc. All rights reserved. Reprinted by permission.

Judy LeSage for "No Matter What Choices You Make in Life, You're Still a Part of Me." Copyright © 1999 by Judy LeSage. All rights reserved. Reprinted by permission.

Hay House, Inc. for "I communicate freely." from MEDITATIONS TO HEAL YOUR LIFE by Louise L. Hay. Copyright © 1994 by Louise L. Hay. All rights reserved. Reprinted by permission of the publisher, Hay House, Inc., Carlsbad, CA.

Barbara Cage for "A Teenager Is... a person who...." Copyright © 1999 by Barbara Cage. All rights reserved. Reprinted by permission.

PrimaDonna Entertainment Corp. for "Accept Yourself" by Donna Fargo. Copyright © 1999 by PrimaDonna Entertainment Corp. All rights reserved. Reprinted by permission.

Barbara J. Hall for "It isn't your background...." Copyright © 1999 by Barbara J. Hall. All rights reserved. Reprinted by permission.

Kelly D. Caron for "Don't Walk Alone Through Life." Copyright © 1999 by Kelly D. Caron. All rights reserved. Reprinted by permission.

A careful effort has been made to trace the ownership of poems and excerpts used in this anthology in order to obtain permission to reprint copyrighted materials and give proper credit to the copyright owners. If any error or omission has occurred, it is completely inadvertent, and we would like to make corrections in future editions provided that written notification is made to the publisher:

SPS STUDIOS, INC., P.O. Box 4549, Boulder, CO 80306.